CHRIST IN YOU ...
GOD'S MANIFEST PRESENCE IN THE WORLD TODAY

A Biblical-Theological Study of
God's Interaction with Man

Dr. Douglas G. Sullivan

ISBN 978-1-64028-048-9 (Paperback)
ISBN 978-1-64028-049-6 (Digital)

Christian Faith Publishing, Inc.
296 Chestnut Street
Meadville, PA 16335
www.christianfaithpublishing.com

Printed in the United States of America

Acknowledgment

For my dear wife, Debbie: You have always been my best cheerleader, constant companion, and forever friend. Just as we promised each other some thirty-five years ago, I will love you always and forever for your never-ending love and faithful support. Thank you for your always practical words of wisdom, your desire to walk with me through times of uncertain change, and your continuous support of my God-given dreams. You are an incredible partner in the journey to which God has called us.

Finally, *thanks to Jesus Christ*, who set the example for me to become the Word of God incarnate to my culture and live out His glory—full of grace and truth.

CONTENTS

INTRODUCTION

This book examines the biblical-theological foundation for developing the necessary understanding of the true incarnational ministry impact of spirit-filled Christians in marketplace outreaches, and it provides hope for believers in the world today by showing that as they develop a true relationship with the LORD, God's revealed glory in them also transforms individuals in their communities. People find the evidence of God's manifest presence in relationships. God connects individually with humans and then impacts His people through personal interactions.

GOD'S MANIFEST PRESENCE

The New Testament Church grew through the exponential power of small groups that allowed God's manifest presence to transform them and help them reach out to other people. One such community of faith in post-modern culture—spirit-filled believers ministering in the workplaces and marketplaces in which they live—must base their approaches on the eternal principles they find in God's Word. Then, with the manifest presence of the LORD and the power of the Holy Spirit working in them, they must carry out a practical theology of evangelism and discipleship to the people to whom God calls them to minister. The church must rediscover the biblical principles of God's glory and presence within His community of faith. But to accomplish this, one must first recognize God's glory and presence.

People who walk with Him and allow His glory to change their lives through a personal relationship with Him experience the manifest presence of God. Desmond

Alexander and Brian Rosner assert that "God's glory is his visible and active presence."[1] Walter Elwell also writes much about the manifest presence of God. He states, "The Scriptures often speak of God's presence in human history. The most common Hebrew term for 'presence' is paniym— פנים, which implies a close and personal encounter with the Lord."[2] *HarperCollins Bible Dictionary* defines God's glory as the "...divine attribute indicating significance, importance, or presence..." The glory of God is sometimes said to appear to people, indicating that God's worth and significance has become particularly manifest. In some instances, God's "glory" seems to serve as a virtual synonym for God's presence or being."[3]

The New Dictionary of Biblical Theology confirms this viewpoint as it continues:

> This *interchangableness* or close association of God's glory and his presence/ face, his goodness, his name and his radi-

1. T. Desmond Alexander and Brian S. Rosner, *New Dictionary of Biblical Theology* (Leicester, England: Inter-Varsity Press, 2000), 508.
2. Walter A. Elwell, *Evangelical Dictionary of Biblical Theology*, Baker Reference Library (Grand Rapids, MI: Baker Books, 1996), 629.
3. Mark Allen Powell, *HarperCollins Bible Dictionary* (New York: HarperOne, 2011), 331–332.

ance...indicates that God's glory is his manifest presence, which without further mediation, will destroy his creatures, but which admits the most intimate fellowship with him. In the NT Jesus Christ is the ultimate and permanent expression of divine glory. God's glorious presence, whether for salvation or destruction, is prominent in the decisive moments and central institutions of Israel's history...the NT explicitly applies such passages to Jesus as the Christ.[4]

Therefore, many scholars agree that God's manifest presence is interchangeable with His glory.

By exploring fundamental biblical texts about the nature of God's glory or presence, scholars encounter a biblical theology[5] for the manifest presence of God in the Old Testament covenants. Specifically, they should exam-

---

4.   Alexander and Rosner, 508.
5.   See Edmund P. Clowney, *Unfolding Mystery: Discovering Christ in the Old Testament* (Phillipsburg, PA: Presbyterian and Reformed Publishing Company, 1988), 8, for J. I. Packer's definition: "Biblical theology is the umbrella name for those disciplines that explore the unity of the Bible."

ine the Hebrew terms for walk[6] (halak—רלה),[7] face or presence[8] (paniym—םינפ),[9] appear[10] (ra'ah—האר),[11] and glory[12] (kabowd—דובכ)[13] in relation to Adam, Noah, Abraham, Moses, David, and the prophets during the exile of Israel.

Scholars can also trace the impact of God's manifest presence in the New Testament by looking at Jesus' incarnation, God's glory in the New Testament Church during these last days, and finally how His glory and divine presence will once again be forever present with humankind in the New Creation. This work explores the Greek term for glory[14] (doxa—δόξα).[15] Their study should also briefly dis-

---

6.   James Strong, *The New Strong's Exhaustive Concordance of the Bible: A Concise Dictionary of the Words in the Hebrew Bible* (1890; repr., Nashville, TN: Thomas Nelson Publishers, 1990), 33.

7.   Francis Brown, *The Brown-Driver-Briggs Hebrew and English Lexicon: With an Appendix Containing the Biblical Aramaic*, new ed. (Peabody, MA: Hendrickson Publishers, 2012), 229–237.

8.   Strong, *Hebrew Bible*, 95.

9.   Brown, 815–819.

10. Strong, *Hebrew Bible*, 106.

11. Brown, 906–908.

12. Strong, *Hebrew Bible*, 54.

13. Brown, 458–459.

14. Strong, *The New Strong's Exhaustive Concordance of the Bible: A Concise Dictionary of the Words in the Greek New Testament* (1890; repr., Nashville, TN: Thomas Nelson Publishers, 1990), 24.

15. Frederick William Danker, *A Greek-English Lexicon of the New*

cuss the Greek terms for walk[16] (peripateo—περιπατέω)[17] and face or presence[18] (prosopon—πρόσωπον)[19] in relationship to a couple of important passages.

Finally, an effective study includes summarizing God's manifest presence incarnated through the ministry of presence in both Old Testament and New Testament examples. It also shows the transformation application which true incarnational service should have to the world when the holy presence of the Almighty transforms believers in local communities today.

Testament and Other Early Christian Literature, 3rd ed. (Chicago: University of Chicago Press, 2001), 256–258.
16. Strong, *Greek New Testament*, 57.
17. Danker, 803.
18. Strong, *Greek New Testament*, 62.
19. Danker, 887–888.

GOD'S MANIFEST PRESENCE IN THE OLD TESTAMENT

Introduction

A biblical foundation for a believer's relational outreach ministry must begin with the glorious nature of God. In creation, the LORD made humankind to walk in His divine glory. God created humans in His image and designed them to reflect the likeness of His glory until Adam and Eve disconnected the relationship to God's holy presence and His glory through sin.

This section explores key biblical texts about the nature of God's glory by examining the biblical theology for the manifest presence of God in the Old Testament covenants. It specifically examines Adam, Noah, Abraham, Moses, David, and the prophets during the exile of Israel in relationship to the glory and presence of the Lord. Scholar William Holladay asserts that this glory is a visible manifestation of the presence of God (the outward appearance).[20] Edward Goodrick and John Kohlenberger note that this term appears 120 times in the Hebrew Old Testament.[21]

In the Beginning ... To Adam

As believers study God's interaction with humans in the Garden of Eden, they discover that the LORD speaks to and walks with Adam and Eve in the cool of the day. His manifest presence is with them. As Genesis 3:8[22] records, "They heard the sound of the LORD God walking in the garden in the cool of the day, and the man and his wife hid themselves from the presence of the Lord God among the trees of the garden" (NASB).

Humankind finds ultimate fulfillment in relationship with God because God desires to connect with them as the significant apex of His creation.[23] God creates Adam

---

20. William Lee Holladay, *A Concise Hebrew and Aramaic Lexicon of the Old Testament: Based Upon the Lexical Work of Ludwig Koehler and Walter Baumgartner* (Grand Rapids, MI: Eerdmans, 1971), 150-51.
21. Edward W. Goodrick and John R. Kohlenberger, *The NIV Exhaustive Concordance* (Grand Rapids, MI: Zondervan, 1990), 1483.
22. All scripture quotations, unless otherwise noted, are from the New International Version.
23. Clark H. Pinnock, *Tracking the Maze: Finding Our Way through*

to bear His image[24] and to have community with Him. Concurrently, God's image bearer longs for authentic relationship with other image bearers. This connection with other humans (individual and small group relationships) is a major way God uses believers who experience His manifest presence to impact the communities in which they live. Building relationships with people where they live is vital for believers to allow God's glory, which they experience, to flow through them to others in the ministry of presence.[25]

There is no specific mention of God's glory or presence in the opening passages of the Creation Covenant, but the man and woman experience the manifest presence of the LORD as He walks with them in the Garden. God creates Adam and Eve to enjoy a personal relationship with Him. After their deception, they try to remove themselves from this holy presence by hiding among the trees in the garden, but God is omnipresent, so their attempt is futile.[26] As time continues, Cain murders his brother Abel, which displeases

---

Modern Theology from an Evangelical Perspective (San Francisco: Harper and Row, 1990), 193–194.

24. Tremper Longman and David E. Garland, *The Expositor's Bible Commentary*, rev. ed., vol. 1, *Genesis–Leviticus* (Grand Rapids, MI: Zondervan, 2008), 72–73.

25. Naomi K. Paget and Janet R. McCormack, *The Work of the Chaplain* (Valley Forge, PA: Judson Press, 2006), 28.

26. Ibid., 88.

God. He disciplines Cain, who leaves the LORD's presence and lives "in the land of Nod, east of Eden" (Gen. 4:16).

These early humans walk with the Lord and personally experience His glory until sin separates them from God's presence. As one examines the progression in the book of Genesis, this pattern continues with a man named Enoch, who God honors by translating him away from the world to be in His manifest presence forever without experiencing death.[27] Enoch walks faithfully with God for 300 years, living to 365. Then "he was no more because God took him away." (Gen. 5:22–24).

Throughout the early chapters of Genesis, God's glory is present and revealed to His people. God reflects His manifest presence in the humans He creates, and His glory impacts those who encounter it as well as the people and places around them.

In the Flood ... To Noah

In Genesis 6, the Bible notes that sin continues to increase on the earth, and eventually the LORD regrets that He has created human beings. So God decides to wipe from the

---

27. Victor P. Hamilton, *The Book of Genesis, Chapters 1–17,* The New International Commentary on the Old Testament (Grand Rapids, MI: Eerdmans, 1990), 257.

face of the earth the human race He created. One man, though, finds favor in the eyes of the Lord, and his name is Noah (Gen. 6:6–8). Genesis 6:9 states, "Noah was a righteous man, blameless among the people of his time, and he walked faithfully with God." The account reveals that the LORD speaks to Noah and his sons and interacts in these people's lives.

In Genesis 9, God delivers Noah from the flood and then makes a covenant with Noah and his sons. Bible Commentator John Walton claims that "[t]his is the first reference to the word 'covenant' (*berit*) in the Bible."[28] Noah and his sons personally experience the manifest presence of God as He blesses them and calls them once again to be fruitful and multiply. He gives a sign in the clouds of His covenant, which He establishes with all life on the earth assuring them of His promise to all humankind (Gen. 9:16). Once again, the evidence confirms that God's manifest presence is among those faithful humans with whom He walks and talks.

---

28. John H. Walton, *Genesis: From Biblical Text... to Contemporary Life*, The NIV Application Commentary (Grand Rapids, MI: Zondervan, 2001), 343–344.

In the Journey ... To Abraham

From the line of Noah's son Shem, God continues inter-acting with the humans He created. In Genesis 12:1–3, the LORD gives a specific call to Abram, the son of Terah, from Ur of the Chaldees.[29] He commands, "Go from your country, your people and your father's household to the land I will show you. I will make you into a great nation, and I will bless you; I will make your name great, and you will be a blessing. I will bless those who bless you, and who-ever curses you I will curse; and all peoples on earth will be blessed through you."

God enters these people's lives and walks with them. His relationship with Abram, who becomes Abraham, is so close that in the New Testament, James calls Abraham "God's friend" (James 2:23). There is no specific mention of the LORD's manifest presence as He interacts with the patriarchs, but one continuously finds that God appears to each of them. In Genesis 12:7, 17:1, and 18:1, the LORD appears to Abraham. In Genesis 26:2 and 26:24, the LORD appears to Isaac, and in Genesis 35:1 and 35:9, God appears

---

29. Longman and Garland, *The Expositor's Bible Commentary*, vol. 1, 148.

to Jacob, who becomes Israel (Gen. 32:28), meaning "he struggles with God."[30]

Finally, enemies carry Israel's son, Joseph, off in bondage to Egypt. The Bible reports in Genesis 39:2 and Genesis 39:23 that the LORD is "with Joseph" as he encounters both good and bad circumstances. God's manifest presence helps Joseph succeed as he walks in relationship with Him. Hamilton explains how Yahweh's presence keeps Joseph from being alone.

> He (Joseph) is alone in Egypt, separated from family, vulnerable, with a cloud over his future. Or is he alone? Only the narrator, never any of the characters, uses the name Yahweh. Thus, it is the narrator who tells us, no less than five times, that in a very precarious situation, Joseph is not really alone. Yahweh is with him. There is no doubt about Yahweh's presence with Joseph from this point on in the narrative.[31]

---

30. Victor P. Hamilton, *The Book of Genesis, Chapters 18–50,* The New International Commentary on the Old Testament (Grand Rapids, MI: Eerdmans, 1995), 459.
31. Walton, 606–607.

So even in distant places, Yahweh's holy presence prospers faithful people like Joseph as they walk in close relationship with Him.

In the Law ... To Moses

As the children of Israel struggle in bondage under the house of Pharaoh in Egypt, God continues to hear their cries and interact in their lives. The LORD calls a man, Moses, to be their deliverer. God reveals His manifest presence to Moses through a burning bush not consumed by the fire (Exod. 3:2). Once again, as with Abram, God gives a specific call to His chosen servant. In Exodus 3:12, the LORD assures Moses that He will be with him,[32] then Moses goes back to Egypt to confront Pharaoh and demand the release of God's special people.

Moses, like the patriarchs before him, walks with God. The LORD's presence sustains him even in times of great discouragement and loneliness. In Exodus 6:2–4, God speaks encouragement to Moses, "I am the Lord. I appeared to Abraham, to Isaac and to Jacob as God Almighty, but by my name the Lord I did not make myself fully known to them. I also established my covenant with them." This

---

32. Walter A. Elwell, *Baker Commentary on the Bible* (Grand Rapids, MI: Baker Books, 2000), 43–45.

encouragement strengthens Moses and gives him courage to fulfill the LORD's mission to free the Children of Israel from Pharaoh.

God shows His manifest presence to Moses and then reveals himself to the stiff-necked people He delivers out of Egypt. As the Israelites gripe and complain in the wilderness, Aaron warns them: "In the morning you will see the glory of the LORD, because He has heard your grumbling against Him." (Exod. 16:7). Then scripture states, "[W]hile Aaron spoke to the whole Israelite community, they looked toward the desert, and there was the glory of the LORD appearing in the cloud." (16:10) This cloud of glory is not only evident to Moses, Aaron, and other faithful followers of the God of Abraham, Isaac, and Jacob, but it is obvious to the entire community as the presence of the LORD begins to do His work in these people. Exodus 24:15–17 explains, "When Moses went up on the mountain, the cloud covered it, and the glory of the Lord settled on Mount Sinai. For six days the cloud covered the mountain, and on the seventh day the Lord called to Moses from within the cloud. To the Israelites the glory of the Lord looked like a consuming fire on top of the mountain." Peter Enns describes how the whole community experiences the manifest presence of God:

God's presence on the mountain is represented as cloud and fire...The significance of the cloud in chapter 24 is not simply another indication of God's presence with Moses, although it is certainly that as well. It is rather another element in the narrative that sets the stage for what is to come...there is a clear connection between Mount Sinai and the tabernacle. Both are where God's glory resides in the form of a cloud...Sinai is not a reflection on the tabernacle but the other way around. God meets with his people at Mount Sinai, and the tabernacle is a way of making that presence "portable."[33]

The LORD speaks to Moses face to face, and Exodus 33:11 reports that it is just "as one speaks to a friend." Moses' relationship with God's holy presence changes his life. As an anointed leader of God's people, Moses depends on this sacred experience to give him both strength and rest for the tasks at hand. According to scripture, the LORD replies, "'My Presence will go with you, and I will give you

---

33.   Peter Enns, *Exodus, The NIV Application Commentary from Biblical Text—to Contemporary Life*, The NIV Application Commentary (Grand Rapids, MI: Zondervan, 2000), 493.

CHRIST IN YOU...
GOD'S MANIFEST PRESENCE IN THE WORLD TODAY

rest.' Then Moses sa[ys] to him, 'If your Presence does not go with us, do not send us up from here.'" (Exod. 33:14–15). Once Moses experiences this personal relationship with God, he knows he needs this manifest presence to be with him forever.

God's glory changes Moses so much that he wants even more of it in his life. He pleads with the LORD to reveal more of Himself in Exodus 33:18–23:

> 18Then Moses said, "Now show me your glory."

> 19And the Lord said, "I will cause all my goodness to pass in front of you, and I will proclaim my name, the Lord, in your presence. I will have mercy on whom I will have mercy, and I will have compassion on whom I will have compassion. 20But," he said, "you cannot see my face, for no one may see me and live."

> 21Then the Lord said, "There is a place near me where you may stand on a rock. 22When my glory passes by, I will put you in a cleft in the rock and cover you with my hand until I have passed by. 23Then I

will remove my hand and you will see my
back; but my face must not be seen."

Throughout Exodus, God's glory appears, in some instances as a cloud or as fire. Powell asserts, "God's glory is likewise associated with the tabernacle and with the temple."[34] So after Moses encounters God's manifest presence, the Lord chooses to be present with His people. Enns explains how Yahweh reveals Himself to the children of Israel:

> God must now "connect" to the people at a distance, in a simple tent … The fact that a temporary tent of meeting is set up … signals to the reader that God has not entirely abandoned Israel. This so-called tent of meeting will soon give way to the splendor of the tabernacle, the true Tent of Meeting. The cloud will soon descend to guide the entire camp.[35]

Not only does His presence and glory change lives, but it even impacts the physical location where it manifests. The place where God meets with His people is "consecrated by

---

34.	Powell, 332.
35.	Enns, 579–580.

my glory" (Exod. 29:43). Exodus 40:34–35 explains how God's presence fills a place and makes it holy: "Then the cloud covered the tent of meeting, and the glory of the LORD filled the tabernacle. Moses could not enter the tent of meeting because the cloud had settled on it, and the glory of the LORD filled the tabernacle." Elwell discusses how the tabernacle of God becomes the place where His glory appears not only to Moses but before all the people of Israel:

> The glory of God had taken up temporary residence in the tent of meeting (33:7–9) and could now relocate to the tabernacle (vv. 34–35). God's glory that had appeared on the mountain during the covenant ceremony (19:16–20; 24:15–18) some distance from the people, will now accompany Israel wherever she goes. God thereby fulfills an important aspect of the patriarchal promise "I will be with you," and cements his relationship to Israel. God's glory would be transferred to the temple when it was built (2 Chron. 7:1–3). That same glory would depart when Judah's sins reached the point where

God's sacred presence could no longer tolerate the situation (Ezek. 10:18; 11:22–23) and the temple would be destroyed. But after the exile when the temple would be rebuilt, God's glory once again would fill the Most Holy Place (Hag. 2:7–9).[36]

This pattern of God's manifest presence appearing to Moses and the people continues through the Torah. In Leviticus 9:5–6, God draws people to His presence so they can behold His glory.[37] The passage states, "They took the things Moses commanded to the front of the tent of meeting, and the entire assembly came near and stood before the LORD. Then Moses said, 'This is what the LORD has commanded you to do, so that the glory of the Lord may appear to you.'"

In Numbers 14:10, 16:19, 16:42, and 20:6, the glory of the LORD continues to appear and impact lives.[38] The children of Israel show the effect of God's manifest pres-

36.   Elwell, *Baker Commentary on the Bible*, 63.
37.   Gordon J. Wenham, *The Book of Leviticus*, The New International Commentary on the Old Testament (Grand Rapids, MI: Eerdmans, 1979), 148.
38.   Timothy R. Ashley, *The Book of Numbers*, New International Commentary on the Old Testament (Grand Rapids, MI: Eerdmans, 1993), 254, 313, 326–327, 382.

ence in their midst[39] in Deuteronomy 5:24: "And you said, 'The LORD our God has shown us his glory and his majesty, and we have heard his voice from the fire. Today we have seen that a person can live even if God speaks with them.'"

As the Israelites continue their journey into the Promised Land, Powell suggests that God's presence in the Ark of the Covenant represents His glory. He states, "The most striking fact about the ark at an early period was that it was a direct manifestation of God's presence."[40] As Israel moves forward in battle and conquest, the priests carry the Ark before them. There are few references to God's glory appearing to individuals during the period of the Judges even though the power and presence of the Holy Spirit is obviously with them.

Elwell points out as God encounters and speaks to His chosen leaders, like Joshua and Samuel, that scripture does not record appearances of His manifested glory as they are documented in the Pentateuch. He asserts that, "Normally God's presence with the leader also implies His presence with the people."[41] However, in 1 Samuel 4:19–22, believ-

---

39. Peter C. Craigie, *The Book of Deuteronomy*, New International Commentary on the Old Testament (Grand Rapids, MI: Eerdmans, 1976), 165–166.
40. Powell, 49–50.
41. Elwell, *Baker Commentary on the Bible*, 138.

ers discover that His manifest presence departs from Israel as the Philistines capture the Ark of the Covenant:[42]

> His daughter-in-law, the wife of Phinehas, was pregnant and near the time of delivery. When she heard the news that the ark of God had been captured and that her father-in-law and husband were dead, she went into labor and gave birth, but was overcome by her labor pains. As she was dying, the women attending her said, "Don't despair; you have given birth to a son." But she did not respond or pay any attention. She named the boy Ichabod, saying, "The Glory has departed from Israel"—because of the capture of the ark of God and the deaths of her father-in-law and her husband. She said, "The Glory has departed from Israel, for the ark of God has been captured.

---

42. Bill T. Arnold, *1 and 2 Samuel: The NIV Application Commentary from Biblical Text—to Contemporary Life*, The NIV Application Commentary (Grand Rapids, MI: Zondervan, 2003), 107–111.

David Tsumura then identifies a pertinent matter to consider. Whose glory disappeared—Israel's glory or God's glory? He elucidates, "For Phinehas' wife, the loss of the ark meant the loss of Israel's glory." But the apparent exile of God's manifest presence (the ark) is not a defeat of God; rather, He continues to show His glory even from exile.[43] So throughout these Old Testament passages, God's glory is still present and evident to His people. His glory continues to change those who encounter it as well as those around them and the location where the encounters occur.

In the Monarchy...
To David and Solomon

As scholars study the Davidic monarchy, they discover that God is still present with His chosen people. The Psalms reveal most of the references to God's presence appearing to King David. David's relationship with the LORD is a unique one. Acts 13:12 calls him "a man after My (God's) own heart." God's interaction with this king vividly reveals His presence. David talks about the joy of God's presence in Psalm 16:8–11:

---

43. David Toshio Tsumura, *The First Book of Samuel*, The New International Commentary on the Old Testament (Grand Rapids, MI: Eerdmans, 2007), 199–201.

I keep my eyes always on the Lord. With him at my right hand, I will not be shaken. Therefore, my heart is glad and my tongue rejoices; my body also will rest secure, because you will not abandon me to the realm of the dead, nor will you let your faithful one see decay. You make known to me the path of life; you will fill me with joy in your presence, with eternal pleasures at your right hand.

Walking in the LORD's presence is important to King David. Gerald Wilson asserts, "Having undergone both inner and outer cleansing as well as a lasting transformation of the spirit, the psalmist can now hope to be sustained by the lasting experience of the presence of Yahweh."[44] After his sin with Bathsheba, David laments in Psalm 51:10–11, "Create in me a pure heart, O God, and renew a steadfast spirit within me. Do not cast me from your presence or take your Holy Spirit from me." David praises God's holy presence even for the beginning of the reign of his son, Solomon,[45] when he exclaims in Psalm 72:18–19, "Praise

44.   Gerald Henry Wilson, *Psalms: From Biblical Text—to Contemporary Life*, The NIV Application Commentary (Grand Rapids, MI: Zondervan, 2002), 776.

45.   Marvin E. Tate, *Psalms 51–100*, Word Biblical Commentary,

be to the LORD God, the God of Israel, who alone does marvelous deeds. Praise be to his glorious name forever; may the whole earth be filled with his glory."

David's son, King Solomon, also experiences God's manifest presence. God speaks to him multiple times, and the LORD uses him to build the Temple in Jerusalem, which eventually houses the Ark of God's Presence.[46] When leaders dedicate this structure, the people encounter God's presence once again as it fills this place:

> When Solomon finished praying, fire came down from heaven and consumed the burnt offering and the sacrifices, and the glory of the Lord filled the temple. The priests could not enter the temple of the Lord because the glory of the Lord filled it. When all the Israelites saw the fire coming down and the glory of the Lord above the temple, they knelt on the pavement with their faces to the ground, and they worshiped and gave thanks to the Lord, saying, "He is good; his love endures forever." (2 Chron. 7:1–3)

---

vol. 20 (Nashville, TN: Thomas Nelson, 1990), 222–226.

46.   Samuel J. Schultz, *The Old Testament Speaks*, 4th ed. (San Francisco: Harper & Row, 1990), 143–147.

Solomon's prayer opens a period of celebration and worship for the children of Israel. God's presence in the temple is revealed by a miraculous fire and the glorious cloud.[47] Later, God reappears to King Solomon and confirms His significant promises to Him as well as reaffirms the promises of the Davidic covenant. Once again, the evidence confirms that God's manifest presence is among those faithful humans with whom He walks and talks.

In the Exile ... To the Prophets

After the reigns of King David and King Solomon, the unified kingdom of Israel divides[48] during the reign of Solomon's son, King Rehoboam (2 Chron. 10–12). The two centuries that follow Solomon are as gloomy as Solomon's era is glorious.[49] But even as evil kings lead the northern and southern kingdoms, the prophets[50] proclaim God's glorious presence and warn the people of the twelve

---

47. Raymond B. Dillard, *2 Chronicles*, Word Biblical Commentary, vol. 15 (Nashville, TN: Thomas Nelson, 1987), 56–59.
48. Elwell, *Baker Commentary on the Bible*, 282.
49. William Sanford La Sor, David Allan Hubbard, and Frederic William Bush, *Old Testament Survey: The Message, Form, and Background of the Old Testament*, 2nd ed. (Grand Rapids, MI: Eerdmans, 1996), 197.
50. Ibid., 221–229.

tribes of Israel. Isaiah, Jeremiah, Ezekiel, and Haggai are just some of the men of God who speak about the glory of the LORD. Isaiah experiences this glory firsthand. In Isaiah 6:1–3, he describes this encounter:

> In the year that King Uzziah died, I saw the Lord, high and exalted, seated on a throne; and the train of his robe filled the temple. Above him were seraphim, each with six wings: With two wings, they covered their faces, with two they covered their feet, and with two they were flying. And they were calling to one another: "Holy, holy, holy is the Lord Almighty; the whole earth is full of his glory."

Isaiah proclaims the glory of the LORD as he warns and encourages Israel concerning the future of the nation and God's plan for their lives:

> The desert and the parched land will be glad; the wilderness will rejoice and blossom. Like the crocus, it will burst into bloom; it will rejoice greatly and shout for joy. The glory of Lebanon will be given to it, the splendor of Carmel and Sharon; they will see the glory of the Lord, the

splendor of our God. Strengthen the feeble hands, steady the knees that give way; say to those with fearful hearts, be strong, do not fear; your God will come, he will come with vengeance; with divine retribution, he will come to save you. (Isa. 35:1–4)

Isaiah foretells that God will reveal His manifest presence to everyone.[51] In Isaiah 40:5, he shares that "all the people will see it together." This holy presence will reestablish Israel and bring healing and righteousness to the nation. Isaiah even says that God's glory will go before them, "and the glory of the LORD will be your rear guard" (58:8). He warns the Israelites that God's glory will rise upon them and appear over them in Isaiah 60:1–2 when he states, "Arise, shine, for your light has come, and the glory of the LORD rises upon you. See, darkness covers the earth and thick darkness is over the peoples, but the Lord rises upon you and His glory appears over you." God's manifest presence is witnessed over them as these prophesies eventually come to pass.

---

51. John N. Oswalt, *The Book of Isaiah*, The New International Commentary on the Old Testament (Grand Rapids, MI: Eerdmans, 1986), 622–623.

Isaiah concludes his message by emphasizing that as Israel embraces God's manifest presence, people will see His glory throughout the world:[52]

> And I, because of what they have planned and done, am about to come and gather the people of all nations and languages, and they will come and see my glory. "I will set a sign among them, and I will send some of those who survive to the nations—to Tarshish, to the Libyans and Lydians (famous as archers), to Tubal and Greece, and to the distant islands that have not heard of my fame or seen my glory. They will proclaim my glory among the nations. And they will bring all your people, from all the nations, to my holy mountain in Jerusalem as an offering to the Lord. (Isa. 66:18–20a)

Jeremiah also calls the Southern kingdom of Judah to repentance. He declares that the manifest presence of God will leave the children of Israel. In Jeremiah 52:3, he reveals an important truth: "It was because of the LORD's anger

---

52. Elwell, *Baker Commentary on the Bible*, 514.

that all this happened to Jerusalem and Judah, and in the end he thrust them from his presence." Jerusalem falls to the Babylonians in 587 BC, and the people destroy the temple after an eighteen-month siege,[53] just as Jeremiah and Isaiah predict. God's manifest presence pushes Israel away from His glory and righteousness.

Ezekiel is another prophet who encounters the glory of God. Elwell notes that Ezekiel is "unique among the prophets"[54] because all of his service to the Lord was conducted outside of the land of Israel. In Ezekiel 3:22–23, he relates his experience with God's presence as well as his own response: "The hand of the Lord was on me there, and he said to me, 'Get up and go out to the plain, and there I will speak to you.' So, I got up and went out to the plain. And the glory of the Lord was standing there, like the glory I had seen by the Kebar River, and I fell facedown." Ezekiel, moved by "the glory of Yahweh, the visible sign of the divine presence,"[55] warns the Israelites that the abominations and idolatry in the temple angers the LORD. He relates another encounter with God in Ezekiel 8:3–4:

---

53. Elwell, *Baker Commentary on the Bible*, 516.
54. Ibid., 559.
55. Daniel Isaac Block, *The Book of Ezekiel*, The New International Commentary on the Old Testament (Grand Rapids, MI: Eerdmans, 1997), 161.

He stretched out what looked like a hand and took me by the hair of my head. The Spirit lifted me up between earth and heaven and in visions of God he took me to Jerusalem, to the entrance of the north gate of the inner court, where the idol that provokes to jealousy stood. And there before me was the glory of the God of Israel, as in the vision I had seen in the plain.

The LORD continues to reveal His holy presence to the prophet. According to Ezekiel 9:3, "The glory of the God of Israel went up from above the cherubim, where it had been, and moved to the threshold of the temple." He reports again, "Then the glory of the LORD rose from above the cherubim and moved to the threshold of the temple. The cloud filled the temple, and the court was full of the radiance of the glory of the Lord" (Ezek. 10:4). This is quite a sight to behold. God permits Ezekiel to witness the "intensification of divine presence represented by His glory" in the holy temple.[56]

---

56.   Leslie C. Allen, *Ezekiel 1–19,* Word Biblical Commentary, vol. 28 (Waco, TX: Word Books, 1994), 155.

Next, the LORD allows Ezekiel to see a vision of His divine presence leaving the temple. The prophet shares this part of the revelation in Ezekiel 10:18–19: "Then the glory of the Lord departed from over the threshold of the temple and stopped above the cherubim. While I watched, the cherubim spread their wings and rose from the ground, and as they went, the wheels went with them. They stopped at the entrance of the east gate of the Lord's house, and the glory of the God of Israel was above them." He continues the account in Ezekiel 11:22–25, as God's presence departs from Jerusalem. He relates,

> Then the cherubim, with the wheels beside them, spread their wings, and the glory of the God of Israel was above them. The glory of the Lord went up from within the city and stopped above the mountain east of it. The Spirit lifted me up and brought me to the exiles in Babylonia in the vision given by the Spirit of God. Then the vision I had seen went up from me, and I told the exiles everything the Lord had shown me.

After the prophet shares this vision with the Israelites in Babylonian captivity,[57] God reveals to Ezekiel that His glory will return to the temple. Ezekiel 43:2–5 reveals that the prophet "saw the glory of the God of Israel coming from the east. His voice was like the roar of rushing waters, and the land was radiant with his glory. The vision I saw was like the vision I had seen when he came to destroy the city and like the visions I had seen by the Kebar River, and I fell facedown. The glory of the Lord entered the temple through the gate facing east. Then the spirit lifted me up and brought me into the inner court, and the glory of the Lord filled the temple."

Ezekiel sees His glory once again. He continues, "Then the man brought me by way of the north gate to the front of the temple. I looked and saw the glory of the LORD filling the temple of the Lord, and I fell facedown" (Ezek. 44:4). Ezekiel emphasizes the fact that Israel will experience God's glory once again.[58] God's chosen people in Jerusalem witness His manifest presence return and inhabit the temple, just as the prophet foretells. Walter Dumbrell asserts that the idea of a New Covenant does not arise among Israel until imminent exile threatens the people. He links God's covenants together as he states, "Ezekiel's restoration

---

57. Elwell, *Baker Commentary on the Bible*, 569.
58. Block, 618.

vision holds forth similar hopes to Jeremiah. The servant embodies the covenant and ensures the fulfillment of the Abrahamic promises and transferral of the Davidic promises to the entire people."[59]

God starts again, reestablishing a covenant of everlasting peace with the faithful remnant of the house of Israel and the house of Judah. Yahweh will live in them; they will be His people, and He will be their God. The prophet, Haggai, also speaks about this event in Haggai 2:6–9:

> This is what the Lord Almighty says: "In a little while I will once more shake the heavens and the earth, the sea and the dry land. I will shake all nations, and what is desired by all nations will come, and I will fill this house with glory," says the Lord Almighty. "The silver is mine and the gold is mine," declares the Lord Almighty. "The glory of this present house will be greater than the glory of the former house," says the Lord Almighty. "And in this place, I will grant peace," declares the Lord Almighty.

---

59. Walter Dumbrell, *End of the Beginning* (Eugene. OR: Wipf & Stock Publishers, 2001), 78.

This passage announces God's intended goal in the rebuilding of His temple. He will establish sovereign reign over the nations and provide the people with the resources necessary to build this new temple and fill it with His manifest presence.[60]

Summary

The biblical foundation for the believers' ministry of presence in community outreach focuses on the manifest glory of God. This section explores key literature about the nature of God's glory by examining biblical theology for the glory and presence of God in the Old Testament covenants. The study examines Adam, Noah, Abraham, Moses, David, and the prophets during the exile of Israel through their relationships to the glory of the LORD. Throughout the Old Testament, from creation to after the exile, literature supports the fact that God's glory is present and revealed to His people. God reflects His manifest presence in the humans He creates, and His glory changes those who encounter it as well as those around them and the places where the encounters occur.

---

60. Pieter A. Verhoef, *The Books of Haggai and Malachi*, New International Commentary on the Old Testament (Grand Rapids, MI: Eerdmans, 1987), 101.

The next section examines New Testament passages to discover that God now reveals an expanded plan for His glory as an extension of what He was already working through the people of Israel to the entire world. Jesus brings His followers into a realm of fellowship with the manifest presence of the Father that will last for eternity. Stanley J. Grenz proclaims, "What begins in the Garden of Eden finds its completion at the consummation of history. God's will for his creation is the establishment of a human society in which his children enjoy perfect fellowship with each other, the created world, and the Creator."[61] But until that time comes, Christ's followers must allow God to reflect His glory in their lives, so they too can become vessels who bring God's manifest presence into difficult life situations and impact the lives of people around them.

---

61. Stanley J. Grenz, *Theology for the Community of God* (Grand Rapids, MI: Eerdmans, 2000), 179.

GOD'S MANIFEST PRESENCE
IN THE NEW TESTAMENT

Introduction

God wants people to experience His manifest presence so that they can be transformed and reflect His glorious image in the world. Humans cannot do that without the work of Christ and the power of the Holy Spirit. So, believers must build effective outreach ministry upon sound biblical, theological, and cultural foundations. Each new generation of spirit-filled Christians must understand and build on these foundations as well as discover relevant contemporary innovations and applications.

This section helps believers integrate an understanding of God's manifest presence in the world with the development of a personal philosophy of ministry by tracing the glory of God in the New Testament through an examination of the incarnation of Jesus, God's glory in the New Testament Church in these last days, and finally the eternal nature of

His glory and divine presence with humankind in the new creation. Elwell emphasizes that this is a visible manifestation of the glory of God and "ultimately that glory would be revealed in Jesus Christ."[62] Goodrick and Kohlenberger claim that this term glory (doxa—δόξα)[63] appears 165 times in the Greek New Testament.[64] The section also explores the Greek terms for walk (peripateo—περιπατέω)[65] and face or presence (prosopon—πρόσωπον).[66]

In the Messiah ... The Word Became Flesh

The epicenter for the biblical story is the Incarnation[67]— God becoming flesh and blood and moving into the neighborhood (John 1:14, *The Message*) in the second person of

---

62. Elwell, *Baker Commentary on the Bible*, 63.
63. Danker, 256–258.
64. Goodrick, 1705.
65. Danker, 803.
66. Ibid., 887–888.
67. The "term 'incarnation' means 'being in flesh,' and is used in Christian theology with reference to the way in which the Son of God assumed a human form in Jesus ... The purpose of the incarnation is accordingly to make the invisible God 'visible' by showing what he is like and how he behaves." For more information concerning this critical Christian concept, see T. Desmond Alexander and Brian S. Rosner, *New Dictionary of Biblical Theology* (Leicester, England: Inter-Varsity Press, 2000), 576–581.

the Trinity, Jesus. The life of Christ gives followers a pattern to follow to know how to be intentionally incarnational in the world so that God's manifest presence is known to others. *The New Dictionary of Biblical Theology* confirms this viewpoint as Alexander and Rosner discuss the concept of the Incarnation in relation to God's glory:

> Through this act God was revealed in a personal way to humankind, and thus in a way which is more adequate for a personal God than revelation through the display of his glory as Creator in the created world (Ps. 19:1) or even through personal communication in the words of the prophets, lawgivers, and the wise. At the same time, it enabled God to be united with humanity and so to bear their sins, die, and make atonement for them in one act of sacrifice and reconciliation. (2 Cor. 5:19–21) Furthermore, through this union of the divine with the human Jesus became the author and head of a new humanity in which those who believe in him are united with him, share in his divine sonship and

become co-heirs with him of glory and participate in the divine nature.[68]

So now, the invisible God is seen through Jesus of Nazareth, so His followers can behold His manifest presence and make a difference in the world in which humankind lives.

Steve Chalke relates the Incarnation even more personally to believers' daily lives: "God comes to where we are, speaks our language and wears our clothes. This central act of all history has huge implications for the way in which we understand and relate to God for the way in which we think of ourselves and others, and for the way in which we imagine society."[69] People encounter God's glory through the Incarnation. Jesus is fully human, and at the same time, He is fully God.[70] Jesus is the manifest presence of His Father. Through His sinless life, atoning sacrifice, death, and glorious resurrection, each believer experiences the Father's glory. The Holy Spirit[71] of God, which lives in believers, makes this possible.

---

68. Alexander and Rosner, 577.
69. Steve Chalke, *Intelligent Church: A Journey Towards Church-Centered Community* (Grand Rapids, MI: Zondervan, 2006), 31–32.
70. Alexander and Rosner, 577.
71. The Holy Spirit of God will be discussed more thoroughly in the next section. For more information concerning how the

The Incarnation reveals God's worldview—His desire that the living Word of God becomes so much a part of every believer that His glorious presence oozes out of them and onto the people around them. The incarnation of Jesus Christ then becomes the prism through which believers view the entire missional task. Christ's attitude should be their attitude when carrying out that mission—that no one is too small, too lost, or too far outside.

With this in mind, believers must understand that God's manifest presence and authority characterizes Jesus' ministry, and Jesus shares this glory and authority with His followers so that they can carry out His mission in the world. As stated earlier, God's Holy Spirit gives Christians power for ministry. Jesus, the Teacher, is God. He personifies the face and community of God incarnate on Earth.[72] Acting as God does not concern Jesus; instead, He cares about touching humankind with God's manifest presence. He interacts with everyone He touches as the embodiment of the holy presence of the Father. Jesus' followers experience discipleship on a completely new level when they come face to face with the living Word full of God's glory.

"agency of the Holy Spirit" participated in the work of the "incarnation," see Alexander and Rosner, 581.

72. Gareth W. Icenogle, *Biblical Foundations for Small Groups Ministry: An Integrational Approach* (Downers Grove, IL: InterVarsity Press, 1994), 117.

Scripture relates, "The Word became flesh and made his dwelling among us. We have seen his glory, the glory of the one and only Son, who came from the Father, full of grace and truth" (John 1:14). Encountering the Father's manifest presence through the Incarnation allows believers to reenter a right relationship with God and accomplish His purpose on the Earth.

Humans can once again relate to the Father through personal interaction with Jesus Christ and the manifestation of God's glory in the incarnation. Jesus reveals himself to His followers and models how people can reflect God's glory in small group experiences. He brings the intimate presence of God back into the supernatural community through His church.[73] Leonhard Goppelt explains how this takes place. He identifies that in creation, "The original Adam may indeed be called a type of the perfect man in the new age."[74] This first Adam experiences a unique association with the presence and glory of God until sin alters the relational picture. The second Adam restores authentic

73. Steven M. Rose, "Breaking the Growth Barrier at Muskogee First Assembly: Facilitating Assimilation and Developing Community through Small Group Ministry" (D. Min. Project, Assemblies of God Theological Seminary, Springfield, MO, 2008), 33–34.

74. Leonhard Goppelt, *Typos: The Typological Interpretation of the Old Testament in the New* (Grand Rapids, MI: Eerdmans, 1982), 33.

relationship with God's glory by giving life to those who believe in Him (1 Cor. 15:22) allowing them to become agents of God in this world to accomplish His work.

This second Adam, the incarnation of Jesus, enters the world He created by the power of the Holy Spirit. He steps into the world as the manifest presence of God the Father, as God the Son, a human being. Angelic messengers proclaim God's glorious presence at Christ's birth. As they share the good news with the shepherds watching their flocks, people once again experience God's glory:

> [9]An angel of the Lord appeared to them, and the glory of the Lord shone around them, and they were terrified. [10]But the angel said to them, "Do not be afraid. I bring you good news that will cause great joy for all the people. [11]Today in the town of David a Savior has been born to you; he is the Messiah, the Lord. [12]This will be a sign to you: You will find a baby wrapped in cloths and lying in a manger."

> [13]Suddenly a great company of the heavenly host appeared with the angel, praising God and saying, [14]"Glory to God in the highest heaven, and on earth peace

to those on whom his favor rests." (Luke 2:9–14)

God now reveals His presence in the flesh to all humans. As Jesus grows "in wisdom and stature, and favor with God and man" (Luke 2:52), He reveals the Father's glory to the people around Him. People who encounter Him every day witness God's presence "in the flesh."[75] Then as Jesus begins His earthly ministry, He reflects God's glory to the Jews at His baptism performed by John in the Jordan River (3:21–22) as God's Holy Spirit descends on Jesus.[76] He accomplishes miraculous signs, which also reveal the glory of the LORD. John records, "What Jesus did here in Cana of Galilee was the first of the signs through which he revealed his glory; and his disciples believed in him." (John 2:11). Each of these events demonstrates to believers how they can also reflect God's glory in their own ministry of presence.

Jesus' earthly ministry lasts three years. During this time, His disciples see many interesting things. One of the most phenomenal events they witness involves the Father

---

75.   Alexander and Rosner, 577.

76.   Darrell L. Bock, *Luke: The NIV Application Commentary from Biblical Text—to Contemporary Life*, The NIV Application Commentary Series (Grand Rapids, MI: Zondervan, 1996), 112–113.

revealing His glory in a conversation on a mountain with two figures from Israel's history, who were also witnesses of God's manifest presence. Luke records this story, "Two men, Moses and Elijah, appeared in glorious splendor, talking with Jesus. They spoke about his departure, which he was about to bring to fulfillment at Jerusalem. Peter and his companions were very sleepy, but when they became fully awake, they saw his glory and the two men standing with him." (Luke 9:30–32).

Elwell, writing about this pivotal event relates, "The purpose of the story (transfiguration) is to confirm Jesus' sonship and glory."[77] Jesus brings forth God's glorious presence in His own life, which He models before His disciples and all the people. The incarnation of God's glory is present, and Jesus wants the lives of those who follow Him to reflect this same glory. Believers ministering in the world must allow this same glory to be replicated in their lives so others around them encounter the manifest presence of God through their ministry of presence.

Finally, as His earthly ministry begins to close during the Jewish Passover feast, He prays to the Father asking to be glorified in His presence before He sacrifices His life on the cross of Calvary:

---

77.   Elwell, *Baker Commentary on the Bible*, 818.

DR. DOUGLAS G. SULLIVAN

After Jesus said this, he looked toward heaven and prayed: "Father, the hour has come. Glorify your Son, that your Son may glorify you. For you granted him authority over all people that he might give eternal life to all those you have given him. Now this is eternal life: that they know you, the only true God, and Jesus Christ, whom you have sent. I have brought you glory on earth by finishing the work you gave me to do. And now, Father, glorify me in your presence with the glory I had with you before the world began." (John 17:1–5)

Jesus desires this not only for His immediate disciples, but for the unity of all believers through the ages to come.[78] He wants people to see the Father's manifest presence in the lives of all who follow Him. He continues His prayer in John 17:20–24 when He states,

78. Gary M. Burge, *John: The NIV Application Commentary from Biblical Text—to Contemporary Life*, The NIV Application Commentary Series (Grand Rapids, MI: Zondervan, 2000), 468–469.

My prayer is not for them alone. I pray also for those who will believe in me through their message, that all of them may be one, Father, just as you are in me and I am in you. May they also be in us so that the world may believe that you have sent me. I have given them the glory that you gave me, that they may be one as we are one—I in them and you in me—so that they may be brought to complete unity. Then the world will know that you sent me and have loved them even as you have loved me. Father, I want those you have given me to be with me where I am, and to see my glory, the glory you have given me because you loved me before the creation of the world.

Believers can be "brought to complete unity" only through a changed relationship with God by the power of the Holy Spirit. Encountering God's manifest presence makes this possible. Christians ministering in local community environments need this unity to provide the spirit-filled ministry of presence which people need in order for their lives to also be transformed.

So, hurting people in the marketplace and workplace can vividly witness God's glory through the Incarnation. Jesus reflects the holy image of His Father. Through His sinless life, atoning sacrifice, death, and glorious resurrection, each person can also experience the Father's glory through the ministry of presence and life of a transformed believer. The Holy Spirit of God, which lives in believers and who will be discussed more thoroughly in the next section makes this possible.

Believers can learn much about how the church should function from one simple fact—God becomes a human. Steve Chalke expands on this idea when he states, "He stood where we stand, shared our world, our emotions, our pain and our humanity. His model for communication is involvement. God does not demand that we meet Him on His terms or on His turf but rather that He journeys to us to meet us on our turf and in our culture."[79] The ministry of presence which believers must share embodies these concepts. Each Christ follower must in turn become the "incarnation" of God's presence to each person in their community if believers are going to transform the world around us.

---

79.   Chalke, 32.

So, the incarnation of Christ establishes the foundation of the church and becomes the pattern for future ministry. God's purpose in the last days is for believers to be intentionally incarnational—to purposely live out and engage the culture of the day. The next section focuses on how that is possible through the power and filling with the Holy Spirit.

In the Last Days ... To His Church

Followers of Christ must understand that the same manifest presence of God and authority that characterizes Jesus' ministry is available to believers today. Jesus shares His glory and authority with His disciples so that they can carry out His mission in the world. God's Holy Spirit[80] gives Christians power for ministry. Jesus cares about touching humankind with God's manifest presence. He interacts with everyone He touches as the embodiment of the holy presence of the Father. George Wood teaches that believers must know the Person of the Holy Spirit for this to take place: "...know

---

80. For more information about the Holy Spirit as the manifest presence of God, see Alexander and Rosner, 551–558, where they state, "As the self-manifesting, transforming presence of God among His people, the Spirit is expected to accomplish deep existential renewal that recreates the very heart of humankind in obedience."

the Holy Ghost—the Holy Spirit—as a loving Person who was already in my life and who was continually seeking to fill me more with the presence of God and make my personality like Jesus."[81] He continues by emphasizing,

> The church cannot function without the Holy Spirit. And our personal life cannot function without the Holy Spirit. We might know a lot about theology. We might study our Bible on a regular basis. But unless we have the operating presence of the spirit in our life, we are not doing anything that really counts in the kingdom of God.[82]

So, Jesus' followers experience discipleship on a completely new level when they encounter God's glory through the Person of the Holy Spirit.

Alexander and Rosner claim the Greek word for church, "*ekklesia*" literally means a gathered assembly. They go on to state, "The church is the temple of the living God and so it should not be destroyed nor defiled ... it is a new

81. George O. Wood, *Living in the Spirit: Drawing us to God, Sending us to the World* (Springfield, MO: Gospel Publishing House, 2009), 29.
82. Ibid., 42.

humanity, taking its origin from the second Adam rather than the first ... it is a body where each member must keep closely in touch with its head." [83] With this in mind, John MacArthur says the following concerning the church: "The coming of the Spirit marks the beginning of the unique church age ... The word 'church' translates '*ekklesia*' which means 'called-out ones.'"[84] These called-out believers experience followership on a totally new height when they encounter God's manifest presence through the person of the Holy Spirit.

The last days begin after Jesus ascends into heaven, and the day of Pentecost is celebrated in Jerusalem (see Acts 2). Stanley Horton teaches that Peter believed this present Church Age to be the last days. He contends, "Thus he [Peter] recognized that the last days began with the ascension of Jesus (Acts 3:19–21). From this, we can see that the Holy Spirit recognizes the entire Church Ages as 'last days.'"[85] While believers are gathered and praying, the Father sends His manifest presence to the church in the form of the Holy Spirit, which Horton also asserts is a person. He explains, "Since the Holy Spirit is a Person,

---

83.   Alexander and Rosner, 407–411.

84.   John MacArthur, *Acts 1–12*, The MacArthur New Testament Commentary (Chicago: Moody Press, 1994), 38.

85.   Stanley M. Horton, *The Book of Acts* (Springfield, MO: Gospel Publishing House, 1981), 38.

we are talking about an experience that brings a relation-ship."[86] Because of this relationship with God's manifest presence, these followers of Jesus are filled with boldness and begin to speak in other languages about "the wonders of God" (2:11). A diverse group of about 3000 peoples' lives are changed as Peter explains what they have just seen (2:14–41).

Carl Brumback parallels this filling with God's Spirit to a similar outpouring during the time of King Solomon: "As in Solomon's day the glory of the Lord filled the temple, so now the Holy Spirit filled these true temples [believers]. They were all filled with the Holy Ghost."[87] MacArthur also discusses this key event: "The evidence of the Spirit's coming was unmistakable. He manifested His presence to the ears, eyes, and mouths of the believers. But it didn't stop there. His coming had a profound effect on the people of Jerusalem as well."[88] So as people witness these things in Jerusalem, many of their lives are impacted and trans-formed by the manifest presence of God working through these believers. Now as God's power becomes available to ordinary, unlearned people, His followers accomplish great

---

86. Ibid., 32.
87. Carl Brumback, *What Meaneth This?* (Springfield MO: Gospel Publishing House, 1947), 17.
88. MacArthur, 43.

miracles and experience extraordinary circumstances (Acts 4:13). However, Jewish religious leaders persecute Jesus' followers.

Leaders put Stephen, one of the early deacons of the church, on trial for blasphemy before the Sanhedrin.[89] He begins his own defense by proclaiming God's glory. Stephen replies, "Brothers and fathers, listen to me! The God of glory appeared to our father Abraham while he was still in Mesopotamia, before he lived in Harran. 'Leave your country and your people,' God said, 'and go to the land I will show you.'" (Acts 7:2–3) The Jewish ruling council, infuriated at Stephen's comments, stone him to death. Scripture relates, "But Stephen, full of the Holy Spirit, looked up to heaven and saw the glory of God, and Jesus standing at the right hand of God." (Acts 7:55)

Stephen, like many others in these last days, experiences God's manifest presence through the power of the Holy Spirit. God's holy presence is now available to Christ's followers as a result of the Word becoming flesh and moving into their communities. The Apostle Paul, another witness of God's glory, experiences firsthand the power of the Holy Spirit and presence of the risen Christ[90] as Jesus encounters

---

89. Elwell, *Baker Commentary on the Bible*, 892–893.
90. Ajith Fernando, *Acts, The NIV Application Commentary from Biblical Text—to Contemporary Life*, The NIV Application

him on the road to Damascus (Acts 9:3–5). He teaches that God's glory is available to all believers in the church through the incarnation of Christ even though human-kind does not deserve it. In Romans 3:22–24, Paul states, "This righteousness is given through faith in Jesus Christ to all who believe. There is no difference between Jew and Gentile, for all have sinned and fall short of the glory of God, and all are justified freely by his grace through the redemption that came by Christ Jesus." All believers have access to God's glory through Christ's incarnation in spite of not deserving it.

Believers in these last days must be witnesses of God's manifest presence,[91] so others should see God's glory in His church through each member. Paul discusses this truth in 1 Corinthians 11:7 as he explains that both men and women in the church experience the glory and presence of God.[92] He continues teaching about this concept in the following passage:

Commentary (Grand Rapids, MI: Zondervan, 1998), 297.
91.   Elwell, *Baker Commentary on the Bible*, 1055.
92.   Craig Blomberg, *1 Corinthians, The NIV Application Commentary from Biblical Text—to Contemporary Life*, The NIV Application Commentary (Grand Rapids, MI: Zondervan, 1994), 211.

¹²Therefore, since we have such a hope, we are very bold. ¹³We are not like Moses, who would put a veil over his face to prevent the Israelites from seeing the end of what was passing away. ¹⁴But their minds were made dull, for to this day the same veil remains when the old covenant is read. It has not been removed, because only in Christ is it taken away. ¹⁵Even to this day when Moses is read, a veil covers their hearts. ¹⁶But whenever anyone turns to the Lord, the veil is taken away. ¹⁷Now the Lord is the Spirit, and where the Spirit of the Lord is, there is freedom. ¹⁸And we all, who with unveiled faces contemplate the Lord's glory, are being transformed into his image with ever-increasing glory, which comes from the Lord, who is the Spirit. (2 Cor. 3:12–18)

Humankind must see God's glory in His chosen people today. Paul states in 2 Corinthians 4:6, "For God, who said, 'Let light shine out of darkness,' made His light shine in our hearts to give us the light of the knowledge of God's glory displayed in the face of Christ." The church possesses this incarnational glory to show others God's presence in the community. God's chosen people must reveal His glory to others as they connect with them on a daily basis. As believers transform into His likeness, their lives reflect His glory.

Elwell relates as he discusses the Father's glory, "[O]nly through Christ can the full light of God's glory become known."[93] But this process of metamorphosis is difficult and discouraging for many Christians. Paul understands this truth and encourages believers in 2 Cor. 4:16–18, "Therefore we do not lose heart. Though outwardly we are wasting away, yet inwardly we are being renewed day by day. For our light and momentary troubles are achieving for us an eternal glory that far outweighs them all. So, we fix our eyes not on what is seen, but on what is unseen, since what is seen is temporary, but what is unseen is eternal."

So as spirit-filled believers focus on God's glory in Jesus, they also have the following assurance: "To them God has chosen to make known among the Gentiles the glorious riches of this mystery, which is Christ in you, the hope of glory." (Col. 1:27) Therefore, believers in these last days are witnesses of God's manifest presence.[94] Paul continues to emphasize this to the church at Colossae when he

93. Elwell, *Baker Commentary on the Bible*, 988.
94. Ibid., 1055.

contends, "For in Christ all the fullness of the Deity lives in bodily form, and in Christ you have been brought to fullness." (2:9–10)

Paul also encourages Jewish Christians to recognize God's presence flowing through Christ and purifying the church to represent the Father's glory to the world. He says, "The Son is the radiance of God's glory and the exact representation of his being, sustaining all things by his powerful word. After he had provided purification for sins, he sat down at the right hand of the Majesty in heaven." (Heb. 1:3) This is when the martyr Stephen beholds Christ's glory. Paul continues, "But Christ is faithful as the Son over God's house. And we are his house, if indeed we hold firmly to our confidence and the hope in which we glory." (3:6)

This is what Paul means when he asks the church at Corinth, "Do you not know that your bodies are temples of the Holy Spirit, who is in you, whom you have received from God? You are not your own." (1 Cor. 6:19) Believers' bodies are sacred and should be treated as holy with God's presence.[95] The Apostle Peter also encourages believers with this truth: "But rejoice inasmuch as you participate in the sufferings of Christ, so that you may be overjoyed

---

95. Blomberg, 127.

when his glory is revealed. If you are insulted because of the name of Christ, you are blessed, for the Spirit of glory and of God rests on you." (1 Pet. 4:13–14) He emphasizes that the Father's manifest presence rests on followers of Christ.

Believers also reveal God's glory by preaching His Word. Sharing God's Word falls into three forms just as the early Apostles proclaim. Herman Ridderbos explains what these three categories are: "Kerygma (proclamation of redemption), Marturia (witness to redemption), and Didache (teaching about redemption)."[96] The people of the world see God's manifest presence as believers proclaim the wonderful deeds He accomplishes. This preaching reveals God's glory.

Edmund P. Clowney concludes that the key to the authority of the message Christians preach is His authority, which reveals this glory. He further states, "This message which was spoken through the Lord has been confirmed to us by those who heard, and their witness has been authenticated by God's miracle-working power."[97] So Christ establishes this foundation of His church as the vehicle for future ministry. God's purpose for the last days is for

---

96. Herman Ridderbos, *Redemptive History and the New Testament Scriptures*, 2nd ed. (Phillipsburg, NJ: P&R, 1988), 50.
97. Edmund P. Clowney, *Preaching and Biblical Theology* (Grand Rapids, MI: Eerdmans, 1961), 53.

His church to function as intentionally incarnational. The missional church of the twenty-first century must once again experience God's manifest presence demonstrating the Holy Spirit as He works through every believer as they boldly share His Word. This is one vital way that followers of Christ are agents who can bring the presence of God into difficult situations.

In the New Creation ... Around the Throne

Jesus teaches His followers during His earthly ministry that God will continue to reveal His manifest presence during the Day of the LORD. He encourages His disciples with the words, "For the Son of Man is going to come in his Father's glory with his angels, and then he will reward each person according to what they have done." (Matt. 16:27) Christ reveals much about the judgment to come when He states: "When the Son of Man comes in his glory, and all the angels with him, he will sit on his glorious throne. All the nations will be gathered before him, and he will separate the people one from another as a shepherd separates the sheep from the goats." (25:31)

Many Old Testament prophets speak of future times in our world, but a great number of their predictions have not yet come to pass. Walter Dumbrell identifies this important issue: "We are able to see that the New Covenant prophesies of Jeremiah, Ezekiel, and Isaiah remain to be fulfilled."[98] According to scripture, separation and judgment will occur. The return of the Lord will usher in judgment which will divide people based on their moral character.[99] Outward proof demonstrates inner righteousness or unrighteousness. This exterior evidence is the result of God's glory working in believers' inward characters.

In Mark 13:26–27, Jesus continues, "At that time people will see the Son of Man coming in clouds with great power and glory. And he will send his angels and gather his elect from the four winds, from the ends of the earth to the ends of the heavens." But He also gives this caution, "Whoever is ashamed of me and my words, the Son of Man will be ashamed of them when he comes in his glory and in the glory of the Father and of the holy angels." (Luke 9:26)

The gospel writer also records, "At that time they will see the Son of Man coming in a cloud with power and great glory. When these things begin to take place, stand up and lift up your heads, because your redemption is drawing near" (Luke 21:27–28). So as the consummation of

---

98. Walter Dumbrell, *Covenant and Creation: A Theology of Old Testament Covenants* (Eugene, OR: Wipf & Stock Publishers, 1986), 184.
99. Elwell, *Baker Commentary on the Bible*, 754.

all things begins, God will reveal His manifest presence as a theophany. Believers must look up with joy, hope, and trust.[100] The Apostle Paul also discusses the glory God will show in the New Creation. He relates,

> I consider that our present sufferings are not worth comparing with the glory that will be revealed in us. For the creation waits in eager expectation for the children of God to be revealed. For the creation was subjected to frustration, not by its own choice, but by the will of the one who subjected it, in hope that the creation itself will be liberated from its bondage to decay and brought into the freedom and glory of the children of God. (Rom. 8:18–21)

The Apostle John, while in exile on the Isle of Patmos,[101] envisions God's glory with the Lamb on His throne in the New Creation:

---

100. Joel B. Green, *The Gospel of Luke*, The New International Commentary on the New Testament (Grand Rapids, MI: Eerdmans, 1997), 740–741.

101. Elwell, *Baker Commentary on the Bible*, 1198.

> Whenever the living creatures give glory, honor and thanks to him who sits on the throne and who lives forever and ever, the twenty-four elders fall down before him who sits on the throne and worship him who lives forever and ever. They lay their crowns before the throne and say: "You are worthy, our Lord and God, to receive glory and honor and power, for you created all things." (Rev. 4:9–11)

In Revelation 5:11–14, as the Father shows him this glorious vision, John then states,

> Then I looked and heard the voice of many angels, numbering thousands upon thousands, and ten thousand times ten thousand. They encircled the throne and the living creatures and the elders. In a loud voice, they were saying: "Worthy is the Lamb, who was slain, to receive power and wealth and wisdom and strength and honor and glory and praise!" Then I heard every creature in heaven and on earth and under the earth and on the sea, and all that is in them, saying: "To him who sits

on the throne and to the Lamb be praise
and honor and glory and power, forever
and ever!" The four living creatures said,
"Amen," and the elders fell down and
worshiped.

John sees the effects of the holy presence of God as "His
glory fills his house."[102] Scripture states, "And the temple
was filled with smoke from the glory of God and from his
power, and no one could enter the temple until the seven
plagues of the seven angels were completed." (Rev. 15:8)
Next, He declares that God's glorious splendor will light
the earth (18:1), and then John beholds God's glory in the
New Jerusalem. Scripture relates,

One of the seven angels who had the seven
bowls full of the seven last plagues came
and said to me, "Come, I will show you
the bride, the wife of the Lamb." And he
carried me away in the Spirit to a mountain great and high, and showed me the
Holy City, Jerusalem, coming down out
of heaven from God. It shone with the

---

102. Craig S. Keener, *Revelation, The NIV Application Commentary
from Biblical Text—to Contemporary Life*, The NIV Application
Commentary (Grand Rapids, MI: Zondervan, 2000), 387.

DR. DOUGLAS G. SULLIVAN

glory of God, and its brilliance was like that of a very precious jewel, like a jasper, clear as crystal. (Rev. 21:9–11)

According to scripture, John also says,

> I did not see a temple in the city, because the Lord God Almighty and the Lamb are its temple. The city does not need the sun or the moon to shine on it, for the glory of God gives it light, and the Lamb is its lamp. The nations will walk by its light, and the kings of the earth will bring their splendor into it. (Rev. 21:22–24)

In this final vision, John proclaims that this city of the New Creation has no need for a temple because as Elwell states, "God's glory is essentially Himself."[103] These examples from scripture reveal God's plan for people to experience His glory in the New Creation. Jesus, the Lamb of God, brings humankind back into a realm of fellowship with the manifest presence of the Father that will last for eternity.

---

103. Elwell, *Baker Commentary on the Bible*, 1227.

Summary

In the New Testament, from the Incarnation to New Creation, people find God's glory present and revealed before His followers. The LORD desires for His chosen people to experience His manifest presence. God creates humans to reflect His glorious image. Sin disconnects people from God's glory, but an examination of New Testament references to God's glory shows that Christ's sacrifice restores humankind's ability to once again partake of His divine presence. John the Revelator proclaims,

> No longer will there be any curse. The throne of God and of the Lamb will be in the city, and his servants will serve him. They will see his face (presence), and his name will be on their foreheads. There will be no more night. They will not need the light of a lamp or the light of the sun, for the Lord God will give them light. And they will reign forever and ever. (Rev. 22:3–5)

New Testament passages reveal God's plan for His people to experience His glory. Jesus, the Lamb of God, brings His followers back into a realm of fellowship with the manifest presence of the Father that will last for eternity.

GOD'S MANIFEST PRESENCE INCARNATED THROUGH THE MINISTRY OF PRESENCE

Summary of Old Testament Examples

The biblical foundation for relational community ministry begins with the glorious presence of God. In creation, the LORD lets humans experience His divine glory. He creates humans in His very image and designs them to reflect the likeness of His glory until Adam and Eve disconnect the relationship to God's manifest presence and His glory through sin.

This Old Testament portion of this book explores key biblical texts about the nature of God's glory by conducting a biblical theology of the glory and presence of God in the Old Testament covenants. The study examines this theme in the context of God's covenants with Adam, Noah, Abraham, Moses, David, and with Israel during the period of prophets during the exile. Throughout the Old

Testament, from creation to the post-exilic era, the biblical-theological literature supports the view that God's glory is present and revealed to His people. God reflects His manifest presence in the humans He creates and His glory changes those who encounter it as well as those around them and the places where the encounter occurs.

Summary of New Testament Examples

Spirit-filled believers build effective community ministry outreach upon sound biblical, theological, and cultural foundations. This writing integrates an understanding of God's glory and presence in the world with the development of personal philosophies of ministry. The study traces the glory of God in the New Testament by looking at the Incarnation of Jesus, God's glory in the New Testament Church in the last days, and finally the way His glory and divine presence will once again be forever present with humans in the New Creation. So in the New Testament, from Incarnation to New Creation, believers find God's glory present and revealed before His people. The LORD desires for His chosen people to experience His manifest presence. God creates humans to reflect His glorious image. Sin disconnects people from God's glory, but an examination of New Testament Scripture shows that Christ's sacrifice restores humankind's ability to once again experience the holy presence of the Father.

New Testament passages reveal God's plan for His people to experience His glory. Jesus Christ ushers His disciples into fellowship with God's manifest presence for all eternity. The power of God's Holy Spirit makes this possible.

Incarnational Transformation Application

When God's glory works in individuals, others around those people witness the changes and see the results of the LORD's impact in their lives. In other words, God's glory begins to move through the first people reaching out to others around them, changing their lives as well. God's manifest presence must be with His people for believers to succeed as ministers of His presence in the local community. God's divine nature is so holy that humans in this present age can only handle limited amounts of it in their lives. There will come a time, however, when people will indeed see Him face-to-face (1 Cor. 13:2).

Over the centuries, the church slowly morphed from engaging culture with God's glory to attracting culture. The missional church of the twenty-first century and current community outreaches must once again become incarnational showing the Father's manifest presence. But this requires great change for most believers. Earl Creps argues that "change usually begins in painful truth."[104] A missionally incarnational version of Creps' statement could read, "Change begins in painful truth, but ends in God's proving and enduring glory and grace."

So today, twenty-first century Christianity has an image problem, remaining stuck in the quagmire of an identity crisis. People know the church more for what it opposes than who it represents. Contemporary culture has a negative image of Christianity seeing the church as a legalistic, dogmatic, self-oriented, and exclusive institution. John MacArthur explains:

> The campaign to make Christianity seem "contemporary" and sophisticated in the world's eyes is proving especially disastrous right now. As postmodern culture becomes more antagonistic to authoritative proclamations of truth, evangelicalism is casually drifting more and more into postmodern ways of thinking about

104. Earl Creps, *Off-Road Disciplines: Spiritual Adventures of Missional Leaders* (San Francisco: Jossey-Bass, 2006), 97.

truth, imagining that this is the way to "reach" the culture.[105]

This is a far cry from the example that Jesus of Nazareth, the founder and cornerstone of the church, lived out while on Earth some two thousand years ago.

Followers of Jesus in the twenty-first century must show the world they are people changed by God—believers who facilitate a deeper, more authentic vision of the church, acting as Jesus' original called-out people changed by and reflecting the glory of a holy God. Unfortunately, the church has grown increasingly isolated from its surrounding community and culture, glorying in a biblical witness it many times has not possessed. Researcher George Barna discusses the declining influence of this modern church on Western culture:

> Research shows that local churches have virtually no influence in our culture. The seven dominant spheres of influence are movies, music, television, books, the Internet, law, and family. The second tier of influence comprises the entities such as schools, peers, newspapers, radio,

---

105. John MacArthur, *The Truth War: Fighting for Certainty in an Age of Deception* (Nashville, TN: Nelson Books, 2007), 48.

and businesses. The local church appears among entities that have little or no influence on society.[106]

Barna describes the need for dramatic change (a revolution) in the church and identifies an important reason for declining impact in society. His research concludes that many church goers have not undergone the life-change necessary to accomplish this mission. He contends:

> A major reason why most local churches have little influence on the world is that their congregants do not experience a transformation in identity. Our research indicates that churchgoers are more likely to see themselves as Americans, consumers, professionals, parents, and unique individuals than zealous disciples of Jesus Christ. Until that self-image is reoriented, churches will not have the capacity to change their world. After all, a revolution is

106. George Barna, *Revolution: Finding Vibrant Faith Beyond the Walls of the Sanctuary* (Carol Stream, IL: Tyndale House Publishers, 2005), 118.

a dangerous and demanding undertaking;

it is not for the minimally committed.[107]

To achieve this revolution, the church must again become a transformed people. Believers accomplish this by allowing God's manifest presence and the power of His Holy Spirit to shine brightly through them and making a difference in other people's lives. This writing provides hope for believers by showing that as they develop a true relationship with the LORD, God's revealed glory in them also transforms individuals in their communities. It is possible to take nominal believers with institutional mindsets and see the presence of God change them into a force that draws other people to deeper relationships with God through the power of the Holy Spirit and a missional lifestyle.

This is not an easily obtainable task. But with God's glory working in them and an understanding of the Holy Spirit's directive, Christ's followers can accomplish this goal. People find the evidence of God's manifest presence in relationships. God connects individually with humans and then impacts His people through personal interactions. Many experts, like Barna and other authorities on missional Christianity, argue it is very difficult to bring about

107. Barna, 87–88.

transformation in a community of believers so individuals can experience this incarnational presence in the way God desires. To do so, the church must return to Christ's example and once again practice and live out a lifestyle of missionality—one in which every believer "seeps into the cracks and crevices of society in order to be Christ (the incarnation of God's presence) to those who don't yet know Him."[108]

Michael Frost and Alan Hirsch assert that God's desire is "to provoke a basic discontent with *what is* and so awaken a desire to move toward *what could be*."[109] Christians living in the post-modern era and understanding the power of God's manifest presence in them must look beyond the moment and grasp the eternal value of what the Holy Spirit is doing in their time. Through the centuries, humankind has fallen far short of God's glory (Rom. 3:23). The task looms large, but through Christ, the goal is attainable. With humans, it appears impossible, but Jesus says, "With God, all things are possible." (Matt. 19:26)

Many scholars agree that God's manifest presence is interchangeable with His glory. However, experiencing

---

108. Michael Frost and Alan Hirsch, *The Shaping of Things to Come: Innovation and Mission for the Twenty-First Century Church* (Peabody, MA: Hendrickson Publishers, 2003), 12.
109. Ibid., 192.

God's glory remains essential in America's current cultural context. Gordon Fee explains, "The early believers did not have buildings called 'churches:' they did not 'go to church.' They *were* the church, and at appointed times they assembled *as* the church."[110]

First-century Christians knew that God's empowering presence transformed their lives. They regularly assembled as small groups in their homes. When possible, they met collectively in large gatherings where they encountered the power of the Holy Spirit with each believer experiencing God's manifest presence as they walked with Him. Scott Duvall and Daniel Hays explain this significant concept:

> The Lord is not something abstract that you feel, but rather a person who speaks, relates, gets angry, hurts, changes his mind, argues, and loves. He relates to his people on a human level, but he continues to be more than us, still above us. He is the hero of the story...However, this complex God has chosen to relate to us personally and to reveal his character to us through these passages. If our goal is

110. Gordon Fee, *God's Empowering Presence: The Holy Spirit in the Letters of Paul* (Peabody, MA: Hendrickson, 1994), 876.

to know God, then it is imperative that
we seek to hear what he is trying to tell us
about himself in these narrative texts.[111]

So, the best way to summarize the transformation
application of this chapter is to put forth encouragement
for believers to be infected with God's glory. The mission
can appear almost overwhelming, but the promise to the
church is "Christ in you, the hope of glory." (Col. 1:27)
God offers hope through Christ's Incarnation to step out of
the box and impact modern culture with God's glory working through His followers. Gabe Lyons offers this critical
challenge: "Every believer must be challenged to become
the kind of Christ followers, friends, and neighbors who
are humble and full of grace, love, and compassion. We
must take the love of Christ everywhere we go and exhibit
an expression of Christianity that seeks to find the good in
all people and point them toward their Creator."[112]

There are no formulas, templates, do-it-yourself pro-
grams, or how-to steps for people to follow. There is, however, a very personal and loving God who desires to accom-

111. J. Scott Duvall and J. Daniel Hays, *Grasping God's Word,* 2nd
ed. (Grand Rapids, MI: Zondervan, 2005), 322–323.
112. David Kinnaman and Gabe Lyons, *UnChristian: What a New
Generation Really Thinks About Christianity... and Why It Matters* (Grand Rapids, MI: Baker Books, 2007), 226.

plish His purpose and reveal His glory in every believer who is willing to let Him. In the quiet places of the heart, He will show the paths He wants every person and assembly of believers to take. In so doing, He lives out His heart's desire among the world.

CONCLUSION

God's manifest glory is incarnated through the ministry of presence in both Old Testament and New Testament examples. True incarnational service should always have a transformational impact upon the world when the holy presence of the Almighty truly changes spirit-filled believers. Biblical-theological literature supports that God's glory is present and revealed to His people. God's manifest presence changes those who encounter Him as well as those around them and even the location where the interaction takes place.

This writing stretches believers' thinking and hopefully implodes some of the embedded theology that has crippled the church over the centuries. In the aftermath of the implosion, the challenge is for every person to examine their hearts and, as a result, pursue the glory of God with greater intensity. For indeed, each believer must truly experience His manifest presence to accomplish the mission at hand.

Bibliography

Alexander, T. Desmond, and Brian S. Rosner. *New Dictionary of Biblical Theology*. Leicester, England: Inter-Varsity Press, 2000.

Allen, Leslie C. *Ezekiel 1–19*. Word Biblical Commentary. Vol. 28. Waco, TX: Word Books, 1994.

Arnold, Bill T. *1 and 2 Samuel: The NIV Application Commentary from Biblical Text—to Contemporary Life*. The NIV Application Commentary. Grand Rapids, MI: Zondervan, 2003.

Ashley, Timothy R. *The Book of Numbers*. New International Commentary on the Old Testament. Grand Rapids, MI: Eerdmans, 1993.

Barna, George. *Revolution: Finding Vibrant Faith Beyond the Walls of the Sanctuary*. Carol Stream, IL: Tyndale House, 2005.

Block, Daniel Isaac. *The Book of Ezekiel.* The New International Commentary on the Old Testament. Grand Rapids, MI: Eerdmans, 1997.

Blomberg, Craig. *1 Corinthians. The NIV Application Commentary from Biblical Text—to Contemporary Life.* The NIV Application Commentary. Grand Rapids, MI: Zondervan, 1994.

Bock, Darrell L. *Luke: The NIV Application Commentary from Biblical Text—to Contemporary Life.* The NIV Application Commentary. Grand Rapids, MI: Zondervan, 1996.

Burge, Gary M. *John: The NIV Application Commentary from Biblical Text—to Contemporary Life.* The NIV Application Commentary Series. Grand Rapids, MI: Zondervan, 2000.

Brown, Francis, S. R. Driver, Charles A. Briggs, and Wilhelm Gesenius. "The NAS Old Testament Hebrew Lexicon." Bible Study Tools.com. Accessed April 5, 2014. http://www.biblestudytools.com/lexicons/hebrew/nas/.

Brown, Francis, S. R. Driver, and Charles A. Briggs. *Brown-Driver-Briggs Hebrew and English Lexicon.* Peabody, MA: Hendrickson Publishers, 2012.

Brumback, Carl. *What Meaneth This?* Springfield MO: Gospel Publishing House, 1947.

Chalke, Steve. *Intelligent Church: A Journey Towards Christ-Centered Community.* Grand Rapids, MI: Zondervan, 2006.

Clowney, Edmund P. *Preaching and Biblical Theology.* Grand Rapids, MI: Eerdmans, 1961.

————. *Unfolding Mystery: Discovering Christ in the Old Testament.* Phillipsburg, PA: Presbyterian and Reformed Publishing Company, 1988.

Craigie, Peter C. *The Book of Deuteronomy.* New International Commentary on the Old Testament. Grand Rapids, MI: Eerdmans, 1976.

Creps, Earl. *Off-Road Disciplines: Spiritual Adventures of Missional Leaders.* San Francisco: Jossey-Bass/ Leadership Network, 2006.

Danker, Frederick William. *A Greek-English Lexicon of the New Testament and Other Early Christian Literature.* 3rd. ed. Chicago: The University of Chicago Press, 2001.

Dillard, Raymond B. *2 Chronicles*, Word Biblical Commentary. Vol. 15. Nashville, TN: Thomas Nelson, 1987.

Dumbrell, Walter. *Covenant and Creation: A Theology of Old Testament Covenants*. Eugene, OR: Wipf & Stock Publishers, 1986.

———. *End of the Beginning*. Eugene, OR: Wipf & Stock Publishers, 2001.

Duvall, J. Scott, and J. Daniel Hays. *Grasping God's Word*. 2nd ed. Grand Rapids, MI: Zondervan, 2005.

Elwell, Walter A. *Baker Commentary on the Bible*. Grand Rapids, MI: Baker Books, 2000.

———. *Evangelical Dictionary of Biblical Theology*. Baker Reference Library. Grand Rapids, MI: Baker Books, 1996.

Enns, Peter. *Exodus. The NIV Application Commentary from Biblical Text—to Contemporary Life*. The NIV Application Commentary. Grand Rapids, MI: Zondervan, 2000.

Fee, Gordon. *God's Empowering Presence: The Holy Spirit in the Letters of Paul*. Peabody, MA: Hendrickson, 1994.

Fernando, Ajith. *Acts. The NIV Application Commentary from Biblical Text—to Contemporary Life*. The NIV Application Commentary. Grand Rapids, MI: Zondervan, 1998.

Goodrick, Edward W., and John R. Kohlenberger. *The NIV Exhaustive Concordance*. Grand Rapids, MI: Zondervan, 1990.

Goppelt, Leonhard. *Typos: The Typological Interpretation of the Old Testament in the New*.

Grand Rapids, MI: Eerdmans, 1982.

Green, Joel B. *The Gospel of Luke*. The New International Commentary on the New Testament. Grand Rapids, MI: Eerdmans, 1997.

Grenz, Stanley J. *A Theology for the Community of God*. Grand Rapids, MI: Eerdmans, 2000.

Hamilton, Victor P. *The Book of Genesis, Chapters 1–17*. The New International Commentary on the Old Testament. Grand Rapids, MI: Eerdmans, 1990.

———. *The Book of Genesis, Chapters 1–17*. The New International Commentary on the Old Testament. Grand Rapids, MI: Eerdmans, 1995.

Holladay, William Lee. *A Concise Hebrew and Aramaic Lexicon of the Old Testament: Based Upon the Lexical Work of Ludwig Koehler and Walter Baumgartner*. Grand Rapids, MI: Eerdmans, 1971.

Horton, Stanley M. *The Book of Acts*. Springfield, MO: Gospel Publishing House, 1981.

Icenogle, Gareth W. *Biblical Foundations for Small Group Ministry: An Integrational Approach.* Downers Grove, IL: InterVarsity Press, 1994.

Kinnaman, David, and Gabe Lyons. *UnChristian: What a New Generation Really Thinks About Christianity … and Why It Matters.* Grand Rapids, MI: Baker Books, 2007.

La Sor, William Sanford, David Allan Hubbard, and Frederic William Bush. *Old Testament Survey: The Message, Form, and Background of the Old Testament.* 2nd ed. Grand Rapids, MI: Eerdmans, 1996.

Longman, Tremper, and David E. Garland. *The Expositor's Bible Commentary.* Rev. ed. 13 vols. Grand Rapids, MI: Zondervan, 2006–2012.

MacArthur, John. *The MacArthur New Testament Commentary: Acts 1–12.* Chicago: Moody Press, 1994.

———. *The Truth War: Fighting for Certainty in an Age of Deception.* Nashville, TN: Nelson Books, 2007.

Oss, Douglas. "Biblical-Theology of Ministry." Class notes for PTH 902 Course at Assemblies of God Theological Seminary, Springfield, MO, February 25-March 1, 2013.

Oswalt, John N. *The Book of Isaiah*. The New International Commentary on the Old Testament. Grand Rapids, MI: Eerdmans, 1986.

Pinnock, Clark H. *Tracking the Maze: Finding Our Way through Modern Theology from an Evangelical Perspective*. San Francisco: Harper and Row, 1990.

Powell, Mark Allen. *HarperCollins Bible Dictionary*. New York: HarperOne, 2011.

Ridderbos, Herman. *Redemptive History and the New Testament Scriptures*. 2nd ed. Phillipsburg, PA: Presbyterian and Reformed Publishing Company, 1988.

Rose, Steven M. "Breaking the Growth Barrier at Muskogee First Assembly: Facilitating Assimilation and Developing Community through Small Group Ministry." D. Min. Project, Assemblies of God Theological Seminary, Springfield, MO, 2008.

Schultz, Samuel J. *The Old Testament Speaks*. 4th ed. San Francisco: Harper & Row, 1990.

Strong, James. *The New Strong's Exhaustive Concordance of the Bible*. Nashville: Thomas Nelson Publishers, 1990.

———. *The New Strong's Exhaustive Concordance of the Bible: A Concise Dictionary of the Words in the Greek*

New Testament. 1890. Reprint, Nashville, TN: Thomas Nelson Publishers, 1990.

———. *The New Strong's Exhaustive Concordance of the Bible: A Concise Dictionary of the Words in the Hebrew Bible.* 1890. Reprint, Nashville: Thomas Nelson Publishers, 1990.

Tate, Marvin E. *Psalms 51–100.* Word Biblical Commentary. Vol. 20. Nashville, TN: Thomas Nelson, 1990.

Tsumura, David Toshio. *The First Book of Samuel.* The New International Commentary on the Old Testament. Grand Rapids, MI: Eerdmans, 2007.

Verhoef, Pieter A. *The Books of Haggai and Malachi.* New International Commentary on the Old Testament. Grand Rapids, MI: Eerdmans, 1987.

Walton, John H. *Genesis: From Biblical Text—to Contemporary Life.* The NIV Application Commentary. Grand Rapids, MI: Zondervan, 2001.

Wenham, Gordon J. *The Book of Leviticus.* The New International Commentary on the Old Testament. Grand Rapids, MI: Eerdmans, 1979.

Wilson, Gerald Henry. *Psalms: From Biblical Text—to Contemporary Life.* The NIV Application Commentary. Grand Rapids, MI: Zondervan, 2002.

Wood, George O. *Living in the Spirit: Drawing us to God, Sending us to the World.* Springfield, MO: Gospel Publishing House, 2009.

About the Author

Dr. Douglas G. Sullivan, an insightful and powerful teacher of God's Word, has served as a lead pastor, college professor, chaplain, and counselor for over thirty years. Dr. Sullivan is a retired USAF officer who continues to serve as a Lt Col in the Texas Civil Defense, where he oversees all chaplain and benevolence ministries. He is also an adjunct professor at the Waxahachie Campus of Navarro College where he teaches religion, philosophy, and orientation. Doug is the Emergency Services Chaplain for the Maypearl Fire Department while also providing hospice and bereavement services to patients, families, and caregivers in the South Dallas area as a spiritual counselor for Bristol Hospice Pathways.

Chaplain Sullivan completed his doctoral studies in pastoral care and counseling at Evangel University in Springfield, Missouri. Doug received his Master of Divinity in practical theology from Regent University School of Divinity in Virginia Beach, Virginia. He also has completed all course work for his MS in counseling and human development from Troy State University in Troy, Alabama.

Doug's many hobbies include gardening, landscaping, hunting, fishing, and restoring antique vehicles. He is married to his high school sweetheart, Debbie who teaches special needs children. They are blessed with two married children: Daniel, a Dallas Texas Police Officer; and Catherine, an elementary school teacher. The Sullivans also have three wonderful grandchildren, Sophia, Ty, and Emma and they spend much of their time spoiling them on their small farm just south of Dallas, Texas.